Classic·
MEDITERRANEAN

Classic

MEDITERRANEAN

Sun-drenched recipes from the shores of southern Europe

INTRODUCTION BY
JACQUELINE CLARK AND JOANNA FARROW

HERMES
HOUSE

This edition published by Hermes House
an imprint of Anness Publishing Limited
Hermes House, 88-89 Blackfriars Road, London SE1 8HA

Publisher Joanna Lorenz
Managing Editor Linda Fraser
Project Editor Zoe Antoniou
Designer Ian Sandom
Illustrations Madeleine David
Recipes Carla Capalbo, Jacqueline Clark, Carole Clements, Roz Denny,
Joanna Farrow, Silvana Franco, Sarah Gates,
Soheila Kimberley and Elizabeth Wolf-Cohen
Jacket photography Thomas Odulate
Production Controller Joanna King

Typeset by MC Typeset Ltd, Rochester, Kent

Printed and bound in Singapore

3 5 7 9 10 8 6 4

For all recipes, quantities are given in both metric and imperial measures, and, where appropriate,
measures are also given in standard cups and spoons. Follow one set, but not a mixture,
because they are not interchangeable.

Picture on frontispiece (left to right): Hummus, Focaccia with Onions and puy lentils.

CONTENTS

INTRODUCTION

The Mediterranean conjures up as many vibrant colours as there are countries in the region. Azure skies, white-gold sands, bright, whitewashed walls, brilliant reds, greens, yellows, purples and oranges are seen in abundance throughout the fifteen countries that surround this beautiful sea. A quick tour will take us from the shores of Spain, to France, Italy, Greece, Turkey, Syria, Lebanon, Israel, and into Africa to Egypt, Libya, Tunisia, Algeria and Morocco. And then to the islands of Malta and Cyprus which are truly Mediterranean, encircled by the sea. Although very different, all these countries share a similar terrain and climate, as well as the sea, and this is perfectly reflected most of all in the essence of the food that is loved by all.

There are some basic ingredients that are used throughout the region, and these have strong historical links. In ancient times, the area surrounding the Mediterranean sea was colonized for various periods by the Phoenicians, Greeks and

Romans, who shared a basic cultivation of wheat, olives and grapes. These, in turn, became bread, oil and wine – three components that are still very important in the Mediterranean diet today. With the building of ships came import and export,

and spices and flavourings, such as saffron, cloves and allspice, were introduced through North Africa and Arabia. These are still popular all over the Mediterranean, appearing in both sweet and savoury dishes. Nuts, too, are an ingredient common to many of the countries. Almonds, pistachios and pine nuts are perhaps the most frequently used.

Fresh fish and seafood have been traditionally dominant in regional dishes. The Mediterranean has hundreds of different species of fish and crustacea that are marketed locally and beyond. Visit a large fish market in any part of the region and you will be amazed at the fantastic variety of fish, many of which are completely unknown, except to the locals and fishermen. Although the Mediterranean sea is tiny in relation to other seas and oceans, and suffers from the effects of pollution and low food supplies, some of the most delectable dishes of these countries still rely upon fresh fish.

Perhaps the most characteristic ingredient, however, is olive oil, which varies in flavour from region to region. Italy, France and Spain produce some of the best, and extra virgin olive oil gives the finest flavour of all, while a mixture of peanut oil and olive oil will produce a lighter dressing. Recent research proves this diet to be a very healthy one. Olive oil, used in cooking, contains a high proportion of mono-unsaturated fats.

A Greek salad and a bowl of olives (right).

Vegetables are the key element to the flavours of the winter time. Pumpkins, Jerusalem artichokes, tomatoes, spinach, peppers and asparagus are just a few of the many varieties of vegetables used to make soups. These, eaten with plenty of bread, provide a filling and nourishing meal on a cold day. Many soups are created using simple recipes, containing pulses such as lentils and chick-peas, or meat for a more hearty meal. There are special feast-day soups, and soups to eat after sunset during the fast of Ramadan.

However, the most characteristic Mediterranean soups are based on vegetables, pulses and, of course, fish and seafood. Fish stew and soups are typically Mediterranean and a varied mixture of fish, such as conger eel, John Dory, monkfish, bass, bream and red mullet, can be combined with aromatic

flavourings such as saffron, herbs, garlic and orange peel to make an intensely flavoured fish stock.

The climate of these Mediterranean countries has ensured that salads and cold dishes have always been very popular. There are plenty of wonderful and, of course, fresh ingredients that are

Fresh figs are enjoyed during the summer (above), while a glass of local wine (left) is delicious with any meal.

combined to produce delicious results. In its simplest form, a salad in France, Spain or Italy consists of lettuce dressed with a vinaigrette, often to be eaten after the main course or before the cheese is served. In addition, there are composed salads, with specific ingredients and a special dressing, that are complete dishes on their own. These include all sorts of foodstuffs, such as olives or goat's cheese.

Desserts also make good use of the abundance of fresh produce. For a special occasion a colourful selection of seasonal fruits such as figs, plums, apricots, peaches, melons and cherries makes a stunning finale. Alternatively, there are many cooked, sweet desserts that can be enjoyed after a meal

or as a snack in the afternoon. These delicacies, such as Halva and Baklava, make use of many of the spices that originally were introduced from the Far East. Traditionally, the ingredients and cooking methods in these sweet dishes served as a means of preservation in the hot weather. Today, they continue to provide a burst of energy on a warm, sunny afternoon.

Meat recipes do not feature so strongly in the region's cuisine. The countryside around the Mediterranean can be quite harsh with no lush fields for animals to graze. Beasts are often slaughtered young, with baby lamb and goat being favourite meats, while cattle are a rare sight. Many rural families used to keep a pig that was slaughtered and the meat preserved to feed them through the chilly winter months. This has inspired the wonderful dried sausages and cured hams which are still popular today all over the world.

Poultry and game have always played an important role in Mediterranean cooking. This is largely due to the dry, rugged and, in some places, mountainous land which does not provide good pasture for cattle. Ducks, and in particular chickens, are more popular and accessible to the poorer people of the region, who often raise them on their own land. Chicken is a versatile ingredient because, whilst having its own characteristic taste,

it also absorbs other flavours easily. It is often cooked with fresh, dried or preserved fruits, or nuts and spices.

Grains and pulses are very popular, with wheat being the oldest and most dominant cereal grown in the region. Although wheat is the chief staple ingredient, centuries of trading have intermingled dishes that were originally associated with one country, such as pasta and couscous. Rice has been central to Mediterranean cookery for over twelve thousand years.

Perhaps Mediterranean food is best described as "peasant food", not in a derogatory sense, but as a homage to the people who have provided us with such a vast and wonderful repertoire of recipes, ancient and new. There is an inspiring array of dishes to choose from that are intricately prepared and flavoursome as well as extremely simple and subtle. Whatever your tastes, bring the shores of the Mediterranean into your home with this impressive collection of enjoyable and delicious dishes.

Lemons preserved in salt, with herbs and spices, can add a subtle, fragrant taste to many dishes – remember to rinse off the salt before use.

9

AVGOLEMONO

This is the most popular of Greek soups. The name means "egg and lemon" – the two most important ingredients that produce this light and nourishing soup. Orzo is a Greek rice-shaped pasta, but you can use any small shape.

INGREDIENTS
1.75 litres/3 pints/7½ cups chicken stock
115g/4oz/½ cup orzo pasta
3 eggs
juice of 1 large lemon
salt and freshly ground black pepper
lemon slices, to garnish

SERVES 4–6

1 Pour the stock into a large saucepan, and bring it to the boil. Add the pasta and cook for 5 minutes.

2 Beat the eggs until frothy, then add the lemon juice and a tablespoon of cold water. Slowly stir in a ladleful of the hot chicken stock, then add one or two more. Return this mixture to the pan, off the heat, and stir well. Season with salt and pepper and serve at once, garnished with lemon slices. (Do not let the soup boil once the eggs have been added or it will curdle.)

CLASSIC MINESTRONE

This famous Italian soup has been much imitated around the world – with varying results. The home-made version is a delicious revelation and is also extremely healthy as it has pasta, beans and fresh vegetables.

INGREDIENTS
1 large leek, thinly sliced
2 carrots, chopped
1 courgette, thinly sliced
115g/4oz whole green beans, halved
2 celery sticks, thinly sliced
45ml/3 tbsp olive oil
1.5 litres/2½ pints/6¼ cups stock
or water
400g/14oz can chopped tomatoes
15ml/1 tbsp chopped fresh thyme leaves
or 2.5ml/½ tsp dried thyme
400g/14oz can cannellini or kidney beans
50g/2oz/⅓ cup small pasta shapes, such
as tubetti or macaroni
salt and freshly ground black pepper
finely grated Parmesan cheese (optional)
and chopped fresh parsley, to garnish

SERVES 4

1 Put all the fresh vegetables into a large saucepan with the olive oil. Heat until sizzling. Cover, lower the heat and sweat for 15 minutes, shaking the pan occasionally.

2 Add the stock or water, tomatoes, herbs and seasoning. Bring to the boil, replace the lid and simmer gently for 30 minutes.

COOK'S TIP
Try and make the Minestrone a day early and refrigerate as this improves the flavour.

3 Add the beans and their liquid together with the pasta and simmer for a further 10 minutes. Check the seasoning and serve hot sprinkled with the Parmesan cheese, if using, and fresh parsley.

CHORIZO IN RED WINE

his simple Spanish tapas dish is flamed just before serving. If you like, use small chorizo sausages and leave them whole. Provide cocktail sticks for your guests to spear the sausages when you serve this dish.

INGREDIENTS
225g/8oz cured chorizo sausage
90ml/6 tbsp red wine
30ml/2 tbsp brandy
chopped fresh parsley, to garnish

SERVES 4

COOK'S TIP
After cooking, the chorizo sausage can be cooled, then chilled for up to 24 hours before using.

1 Prick the chorizo sausage(s) in several places with a fork and place them in a saucepan with the red wine. Bring to the boil, lower the heat, then cover and simmer gently for 15 minutes. Remove from the heat and leave the sausage(s) to cool in the covered pan for 2 hours.

2 Remove the chorizo sausage(s) from the pan and reserve the wine.

3 Using a sharp knife, cut the chorizo sausage(s) into 1cm/½in slices.

4 Heat the chorizo slices in a heavy-based frying pan, then pour over the brandy and light it very carefully with a match. When the flames have died down, add the reserved wine and cook for 2–3 minutes until it is piping hot. Serve garnished with chopped parsley.

TARAMASALATA

This Turkish and Greek speciality makes an excellent starter when served with warm pitta bread.

INGREDIENTS
115g/4oz smoked mullet roe
2 garlic cloves, crushed
30ml/2 tbsp grated onion
60ml/4 tbsp olive oil
4 slices white bread, crusts removed
juice of 2 lemons
30ml/2 tbsp water or milk
paprika, to garnish (optional)

SERVES 4

1 Place the smoked mullet roe, garlic, onion, olive oil, bread and lemon juice in a blender or food processor and process until smooth.

2 Add the water or milk and process the mixture again for a few seconds. (This will give the taramasalata a creamier and richer taste.)

3 Pour the taramasalata into a serving bowl, cover it with clear film and chill for 1–2 hours. Just before serving, sprinkle over a little paprika, if liked.

COOK'S TIP
Since the roe of grey mullet is rather expensive, smoked cod's roe is often used in its place for this dish. It is paler than the burnt-orange colour of mullet roe but it is still a very good option.

HUMMUS

Although this popular dip is widely available in supermarkets, nothing compares with the delicious home-made version.

INGREDIENTS
175g/6oz/1 cup cooked chick-peas
120ml/4fl oz/½ cup tahini paste
3 garlic cloves
juice of 2 lemons
45–60ml/3–4 tbsp water
salt and freshly ground black pepper
fresh radishes, to serve

FOR THE GARNISH
15ml/1 tbsp olive oil
15ml/1 tbsp finely chopped fresh parsley
2.5ml/½ tsp paprika
4 black olives

SERVES 4–6

COOK'S TIP
Canned chick-peas can be used for hummus. Drain and rinse them under cold water before processing.

1 Place the chick-peas, tahini paste, garlic, lemon juice, seasoning and a little of the water in a blender or food processor. Begin to process the mixture until smooth, adding a little more water, if necessary.

2 Alternatively, if you do not have access to a blender or food processor, mix the ingredients together in a small bowl until smooth in consistency.

3 Spoon the mixture into a shallow dish. Make a dent in the middle and pour the olive oil into it. Garnish with parsley, paprika and olives and serve with radishes.

SESAME BREADSTICKS

readsticks are a popular addition to many Mediterranean meals and are also delicious snacks. Try serving them with hummus or simply accompanied by a glass of red wine for dipping them into.

INGREDIENTS
225g/8oz/2 cups strong white flour
5ml/1 tsp salt
10g/¼oz easy-blend dried yeast
30ml/2 tbsp sesame seeds
30ml/2 tbsp olive oil

MAKES 30

1 Preheat the oven to 230°C/450°F/Gas 8. Sift the flour into a mixing bowl. Stir in the salt, yeast and sesame seeds and make a well in the centre.

2 Add the olive oil to the flour mixture with enough warm water to make a firm dough. Turn the dough on to a lightly floured surface and knead for 5–10 minutes until it is smooth and elastic.

3 Rub some oil on to the surface of the dough. Return it to the clean bowl and cover with a clean dish towel. Leave it to rise in a warm place for 40 minutes, or until it has doubled in size.

4 Punch down the dough, then knead it lightly until smooth. Pull off small balls of dough, then use your hands to roll out each ball on a lightly floured surface to a thin sausage about 25cm/10in long.

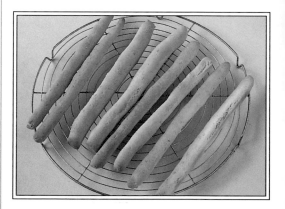

5 Place the breadsticks on baking sheets and bake for 15 minutes until crisp and golden. Cool the breadsticks on a wire rack, then store them in an airtight container until ready to serve.

FRENCH GOAT'S CHEESE SALAD

ere is the French salad and cheese course all on one plate. You could serve it as a quick and satisfying starter or a light lunch. The tangy flavour of goat's cheese contrasts wonderfully with the mild salad leaves.

INGREDIENTS
*200g/7oz bag prepared mixed
salad leaves
4 rashers back bacon
115g/4oz full fat goat's cheese
16 thin slices crusty white bread*

FOR THE DRESSING
*60ml/4 tbsp olive oil
15ml/1 tbsp tarragon vinegar
10ml/2 tsp walnut oil
5ml/1 tsp Dijon mustard
5ml/1 tsp wholegrain mustard*

SERVES 4

1 Preheat the grill to a medium heat. Rinse and dry the salad leaves, then arrange them in four individual bowls. Place the ingredients for the dressing in a screw-topped jar, shake together well and reserve.

2 Lay the bacon rashers on a board, then stretch them with the back of a knife and cut each one into four. Roll each piece up and grill for 2–3 minutes.

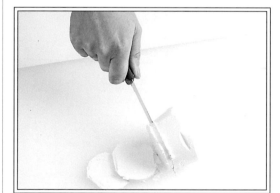

3 Slice the goat's cheese into eight and halve each slice. Top each slice of bread with a piece of goat's cheese and place under the grill. Turn over the bacon and continue cooking with the toasts until the cheese is golden and bubbling.

4 Arrange the bacon rolls and toasts on top of the prepared salad leaves, shake the dressing well and pour a little dressing over each one.

COOK'S TIP
If you prefer, just slice the goat's cheese and place it on toasted crusty white bread. Or use wholemeal toast for a deliciously nutty flavour. Vegetarians can replace the bacon rolls with halved cherry tomatoes, for an alternative juicy flavour.

ROASTED PEPPERS WITH TOMATOES AND ARTICHOKES

his is a Sicilian-style salad, using some typical ingredients from the Italian island. The flavour improves if the salad is made two hours early.

INGREDIENTS
1 red pepper
1 yellow pepper
1 green pepper
4 sun-dried tomatoes in oil, drained
4 ripe plum tomatoes, sliced
2 cans artichokes, drained and chopped
15ml/1 tbsp capers, drained
15ml/1 tbsp pine nuts
1 garlic clove, very thinly sliced

FOR THE DRESSING
75ml/5 tbsp extra virgin olive oil
15ml/1 tbsp balsamic vinegar
5ml/1 tsp lemon juice
chopped fresh mixed herbs
salt and freshly ground black pepper

SERVES 4

1 Cut the peppers in half and remove the seeds and stalks. Cut into quarters and cook, skin-side up, under a hot grill until the skin chars. Transfer to a bowl and cover with a plate. Leave to cool then peel them (*right*) and cut into strips.

2 Thinly slice the sun-dried tomatoes. Arrange the peppers and fresh tomatoes on a serving dish and scatter over the artichokes, sun-dried tomatoes, capers, pine nuts and garlic.

3 To make the dressing, mix together the olive oil, balsamic vinegar, lemon juice and chopped herbs and season with salt and pepper to taste. Pour over the salad just before serving.

CLASSIC POTATO TORTILLA

A traditional Spanish tortilla contains potatoes and onions. Whilst other ingredients can be added to the basic egg mixture, it is generally accepted that this classic tortilla is one that cannot be improved upon.

INGREDIENTS
450g/1lb small waxy potatoes, peeled
1 Spanish onion
45ml/3 tbsp vegetable oil
4 eggs
salt and freshly ground black pepper
flat leaf parsley, to garnish

SERVES 6

1 Cut the potatoes into thin slices and the onion into rings.

2 Heat about 30ml/2 tbsp of the oil in a 20cm/8in heavy-based frying pan. Add the sliced potatoes and the onion rings and cook over a low heat for about 10 minutes until the potatoes are just tender. Remove from the heat.

3 In a large mixing bowl, beat together the eggs with a little salt and freshly ground black pepper. Stir in the cooked sliced potatoes and onion rings.

4 Heat the remaining oil in the frying pan and pour in the potato and egg mixture. Cook very gently for 5–8 minutes until the mixture is almost set.

5 Place a large plate upside-down over the pan, invert the tortilla on to the plate and then slide it back into the pan. Cook for 2–3 minutes more until the underside of the tortilla is golden brown. Cut into wedges and serve, garnished with flat leaf parsley.

SPINACH AND CHEESE PIES

 hese pies are a Greek speciality and are called *Spanakopites*. The strong taste of the feta cheese brings zest to the subtle spinach flavour.

INGREDIENTS
15ml/1 tbsp olive oil
1 small onion, finely chopped
*275g/10oz fresh spinach, well washed
and stalks removed*
50g/2oz/4 tbsp butter, melted
*4 sheets of filo pastry (about
45 x 25cm/18 x 10in)*
1 egg
good pinch of grated nutmeg
75g/3oz/³/4 cup crumbled feta cheese
15ml/1 tbsp grated Parmesan cheese
salt and freshly ground black pepper

MAKES 4

1 Preheat the oven to 190°C/375°F/Gas 5. Heat the oil in a pan, add the onion and fry gently for 5–6 minutes, until softened.

2 Add the spinach leaves. Cook, stirring continuously until the spinach has wilted and some of the liquid has evaporated. Leave to cool in the pan.

3 Brush four 10cm/4in diameter loose-based tartlet pans with some melted butter. Take two sheets of the filo pastry and cut each into eight 11cm/4¹/₂in squares. Keep the remaining filo sheets covered.

4 Brush four squares at a time with melted butter. Line the first tartlet pan with one square, gently easing it into the base and up the sides. Leave the edges overhanging.

5 Place the remaining three buttered squares on top of the first, turning them so the corners form a star shape. Repeat for the remaining tartlets.

6 Beat the egg with the nutmeg and seasoning, then stir in the cheeses and spinach. Divide the mixture between the pans and level smooth. Fold the overhanging pastry back over the filling.

7 Cut one of the remaining sheets of pastry into eight 10cm/4in rounds. Brush with butter and place two on top of each tartlet. Press around the edges to seal. Brush the remaining sheet of pastry with butter and cut into strips. Gently twist each strip and place on top of the tartlets. Leave to stand for 5 minutes, then bake for 30–35 minutes, until golden. Serve hot or cold.

TABBOULEH

This classic Lebanese salad is very popular in many Mediterranean countries. It makes an ideal substitute for a rice dish on a buffet table and is also excellent with cold sliced lamb.

INGREDIENTS
175g/6oz/1 cup fine bulgur wheat
juice of 1 lemon
45ml/3 tbsp olive oil
60ml/4 tbsp fresh parsley, finely chopped
45ml/3 tbsp fresh mint, chopped
4–5 spring onions, chopped
1 green pepper, seeded and sliced
salt and freshly ground black pepper
2 large tomatoes, diced, and
black olives, to garnish

SERVES 4

1 Put the bulgur wheat in a bowl. Add enough cold water to cover the wheat and let it stand for at least 30 minutes and up to 2 hours.

2 Drain the bulgur wheat and squeeze it with your hands to remove any excess water. (The wheat will swell to double the size.) Spread it out on kitchen paper to allow the wheat to dry completely.

3 Place the bulgur wheat in a large mixing bowl, add the lemon juice, olive oil and a little salt and pepper to taste. Allow the mixture to stand for 1–2 hours, if possible, in order for all the flavours in the salad to develop fully.

4 Add the chopped parsley, mint, spring onions and pepper and mix well. Garnish with diced tomatoes and olives and serve.

RATATOUILLE

A highly versatile vegetable stew from Provence, ratatouille is delicious hot or cold, on its own or with eggs, pasta, fish or meat – particularly roast lamb.

INGREDIENTS

2 large aubergines, roughly chopped
4 courgettes, roughly chopped
150ml/¼ pint/⅔ cup olive oil
2 onions, sliced
2 garlic cloves, chopped
1 large red pepper, seeded and
roughly chopped
2 large yellow peppers, seeded and
roughly chopped
fresh rosemary sprig
fresh thyme sprig
5ml/1 tsp coriander seeds, crushed
3 plum tomatoes, skinned, seeded
and chopped
8 basil leaves, torn
salt and freshly ground black pepper
fresh parsley or basil sprigs, to garnish

SERVES 4

1 Sprinkle the aubergines and courgettes with salt, then place in a colander with a plate and a weight on top to extract the bitter juices. Leave to stand for 30 minutes.

2 Heat the olive oil in a large pan. Add the onions, fry for 6–7 minutes, until soft, then add the garlic and cook for 2 minutes.

3 Rinse the aubergines and courgettes and pat dry. Add to the saucepan with the peppers, increase the heat and sauté until the peppers are just turning brown.

4 Add the herbs and coriander seeds, then cover the pan and cook the vegetables gently for about 40 minutes.

5 Add the tomatoes and season well. Cook gently for a further 10 minutes, until the vegetables are soft but not too mushy. Remove the sprigs of herbs. Stir in the torn basil leaves and adjust the seasoning. Serve the dish warm or cold, garnished with sprigs of fresh parsley or basil.

GREEK STUFFED VEGETABLES

Vegetables such as peppers make wonderful containers for savoury fillings. Instead of sticking to one type of vegetable, follow the Greeks' example and serve an interesting selection. Thick, creamy Greek-style yogurt is the ideal accompaniment for this dish.

INGREDIENTS
1 aubergine
1 large green pepper
2 large tomatoes
1 large onion, chopped
2 garlic cloves, crushed
45ml/3 tbsp olive oil
200g/7oz/1 cup brown rice
600ml/1 pint/2½ cups stock
75g/3oz/¾ cup pine nuts
50g/2oz/⅓ cup currants
45ml/3 tbsp fresh dill, chopped
45ml/3 tbsp fresh parsley, chopped
15ml/1 tbsp fresh mint, chopped
extra olive oil, to sprinkle
salt and freshly ground black pepper
Greek-style yogurt, to serve
fresh sprigs of dill, to garnish

SERVES 3–6

1 Halve the aubergine, scoop out the flesh with a sharp knife and chop it finely. Salt the insides well and leave to drain upside down for 20 minutes while you prepare the other ingredients.

2 Halve the pepper and seed and core it. Cut the tops from the tomatoes, scoop out the insides and chop roughly along with the tomato tops.

3 Fry the chopped onion, garlic and chopped aubergine in the olive oil for about 10 minutes, then stir in the rice and cook for 2 minutes more.

4 Add the tomato flesh, stock, pine nuts, currants and seasoning. Bring to the boil, cover and simmer for 15 minutes, then stir in the fresh herbs.

5 Blanch the aubergine and green pepper halves in boiling water for about 3 minutes, then drain them upside down.

6 Spoon the rice filling into all six vegetable "containers" and place them on a lightly greased ovenproof shallow dish.

7 Heat the oven to 190°C/375°F/Gas 5. Drizzle some olive oil over the vegetables and bake them for 25–30 minutes. Serve hot, topped with spoonfuls of Greek-style yogurt and garnished with dill sprigs.

SALAD NIÇOISE

ade with good-quality ingredients, this salad from Provence makes an unbeatable summer lunch or supper dish. Serve with country-style bread and chilled white wine.

INGREDIENTS
115g/4oz/1 cup French beans
12 small new or salad potatoes
90ml/6 tbsp olive oil
30ml/2 tbsp tarragon vinegar
5ml/1 tsp tarragon or Dijon mustard
1 small garlic clove, crushed
30ml/2 tbsp pine nuts
3–4 Little Gem lettuces, roughly chopped
200g/7oz can tuna in oil, drained
6 anchovy fillets, halved lengthways
12 black olives, stoned
4 tomatoes, chopped
4 spring onions, finely chopped
10ml/2 tsp capers
2 hard-boiled eggs, chopped
salt and freshly ground black pepper
warm crusty bread, to serve (optional)

SERVES 4

1 Cook the French beans and potatoes in separate pans of boiling salted water until just tender. Drain well and set aside.

2 Mix the olive oil, tarragon vinegar, mustard, garlic and seasoning with a wooden spoon in a mixing bowl.

3 Meanwhile, toast the pine nuts in a small frying pan until lightly browned. Keep warm till needed.

4 Put the lettuce, tuna, anchovies, olives, tomatoes, spring onion, vegetables and capers in a salad bowl. Pour on the dressing.

5 Sprinkle the warm pine nuts over the salad, add the eggs and toss well. Serve with chunks of crusty bread, if liked.

GREEK SALAD

Anyone who has spent a holiday in Greece will have eaten a version of this salad – the Greek equivalent of a mixed salad. Its success relies on using the freshest of ingredients and a good olive oil.

INGREDIENTS
1 small cos lettuce, sliced
450g/1lb well-flavoured tomatoes, cut into eighths
1 cucumber, seeded and chopped
200g/7oz feta cheese, crumbled
4 spring onions, sliced
50g/2oz/½ cup black olives, stoned and halved

FOR THE DRESSING
90ml/6 tbsp good olive oil
25ml/1½ tbsp lemon juice
salt and freshly ground black pepper

SERVES 6

1 Put the lettuce, chopped tomatoes and cucumber, cheese, spring onion and olives into a large salad bowl.

2 Whisk together the olive oil and lemon juice, then season with salt and freshly ground black pepper. Pour this dressing over the ingredients in the salad bowl and mix them together well but gently. Serve the salad immediately.

RISOTTO WITH ASPARAGUS

isotto is a popular Italian dish and this version is a good choice to make when asparagus is in season.

INGREDIENTS
225g/8oz fresh asparagus, lower stalks peeled
750ml/1¼ pints/3 cups vegetable or meat stock, preferably home-made
65g/2½oz/5 tbsp butter
1 small onion, finely chopped
400g/14oz/2 cups risotto rice, such as arborio
75g/3oz/¾ cup freshly grated Parmesan cheese
salt and freshly ground black pepper

SERVES 4–5

1 Bring a large saucepan of water to the boil and add the asparagus. Bring the water back to the boil, and blanch for about 5 minutes. Lift the asparagus out, reserving the cooking water. Rinse the asparagus under cold water and drain. Cut the asparagus diagonally into 4cm/1½in pieces. Keep the tip and next-highest sections separate from the stalk sections.

2 Place the vegetable or meat stock in a large saucepan, then measure out 900ml/1½ pints/3¾ cups of the asparagus cooking water, and add it to the stock in the pan. Heat the liquid to simmering and keep it hot until it is needed.

3 Heat two-thirds of the butter in a large heavy-based frying pan or casserole. Add the onion and cook until it is soft and golden. Stir in all the asparagus except the top two sections. Cook for 2–3 minutes. Add the rice, mixing well to coat it with butter, and cook for 1–2 minutes.

COOK'S TIP
Risottos have a distinctive creamy texture that is achieved by using arborio rice, a short-grain rice that absorbs plenty of stock, but retains its texture well.

---

4 Stir in half a ladleful of the hot liquid. Using a wooden spoon, stir constantly until the liquid has been absorbed or has evaporated. Add another half ladleful of the liquid, and stir again until it has been absorbed. Continue stirring and adding the liquid, a little at a time, for 10 minutes. Season to taste.

5 Add the remaining asparagus sections to the pan, and continue cooking, stirring and adding the liquid until the rice is tender but still firm to the bite. The total cooking time of the risotto may take from about 20–30 minutes and the amount of liquid needed may vary slightly.

6 Remove the risotto pan from the heat and carefully stir in the remaining butter and the Parmesan cheese. Grind in a little fresh black pepper, and taste once more before adding salt. Serve at once.

FOCACCIA WITH ONIONS

his appetizing flatbread can be split and filled with prosciutto or cheese for an unusual sandwich.

INGREDIENTS
25g/1oz fresh yeast
400g/14oz/3½ cups strong
plain flour
10ml/2 tsp salt
105ml/7 tbsp olive oil
1 onion, sliced very thinly and cut
into short lengths
2.5ml/½ tsp fresh thyme leaves
coarse sea salt

SERVES 6–8 AS A SIDE DISH

1 Dissolve the yeast in 120ml/4fl oz/½cup warm water. Allow to stand for about 10 minutes. Sift the flour into a large bowl, make a well in the centre, and add the yeast, salt and 30ml/2 tbsp of the oil. Mix in the flour and add more water to make a dough.

2 Turn out on to a floured surface and knead the dough for about 10 minutes, until smooth and elastic. Return to the bowl, cover with a cloth, and leave to rise in a warm place for 2–2½ hours, until the dough has doubled in bulk.

3 Knock back the dough and knead again for 3–4 minutes. Brush a large shallow baking pan with 15ml/1 tbsp of the oil. Place the dough in the pan, and use your fingers to press it into an even layer 2.5cm/1in thick. Cover the dough with a cloth, and leave to rise in a warm place for 30 minutes.

4 Preheat the oven to 200°C/400°F/Gas 6. While the focaccia dough is rising, heat 45ml/3 tbsp of the oil in a medium frying pan. Add the onion, and cook over a low heat until soft. Stir in the thyme leaves.

5 Just before baking, use your fingers to press rows of light indentations into the surface of the focaccia. Brush with the remaining oil.

6 Spread the cooked onions evenly over the top of the flatbread and sprinkle lightly with some coarse salt. Bake the loaf for about 25 minutes, or until golden brown. Remove from the oven and cool slightly.

7 Cut the bread into squares or wedges and serve with a meal or on its own, either warm or at room temperature.

OLIVE BREAD

Olive breads are popular all over the Mediterranean. For this Greek recipe, use rich oily olives or those marinated in herbs rather than canned ones.

INGREDIENTS
2 red onions, thinly sliced
30ml/2 tbsp olive oil
225g/8oz/1⅓ cups black or green
olives, stoned
750g/1¾lb/7 cups strong plain flour
7.5ml/1½ tsp salt
20ml/4 tsp easy-blend dried yeast
45ml/3 tbsp each roughly chopped
parsley and coriander or mint
feta cheese, to serve (optional)

MAKES 2 X 675G/1½LB LOAVES

1 Fry the onions in the oil until soft. Roughly chop the olives.

2 Put the flour, salt, yeast and parsley, coriander or mint in a large bowl with the olives and fried onions and pour in 475ml/16fl oz/2 cups hand-hot water.

3 Mix to a dough using a round-bladed knife, adding a little more water if the mixture feels dry.

4 Turn out on to a lightly floured surface and knead for about 10 minutes. Put in a clean bowl, cover with clear film and leave in a warm place until doubled in bulk.

5 Preheat the oven to 220°C/425°F/Gas 7. Lightly grease two baking sheets. Turn the dough on to a floured surface and cut it in half. Shape the dough into two rounds and place on the baking sheets. Cover loosely with lightly oiled clear film and leave until doubled in size.

6 Slash the tops of the loaves with a knife and then bake them for 40 minutes, or until the loaves sound hollow when tapped on the bottom. Transfer them to a wire rack to cool. Serve with feta cheese, if liked.

33

BOUILLABAISSE

Different variations of this French fish stew are found along the Mediterranean coast. Almost any fish and shellfish can be used.

INGREDIENTS

2.7kg/6lb white fish, such as sea bass, snapper or monkfish, filleted and skinned
45ml/3 tbsp extra virgin olive oil
grated rind of 1 orange
1 garlic clove, very finely chopped
pinch of saffron threads
30ml/2 tbsp pastis
1 small fennel bulb, finely chopped
1 large onion, finely chopped
2.4 litres/4 pints/10 cups well-flavoured fish stock
225g/8oz small new potatoes, sliced
900g/2lb large raw Mediterranean prawns, peeled
croûtons, to serve

FOR THE ROUILLE

25g/1oz/²/₃ cup soft white breadcrumbs
1–2 garlic cloves, very finely chopped
¹/₂ red pepper, roasted
5ml/1 tsp tomato purée
120ml/4fl oz/¹/₂ cup extra virgin olive oil

SERVES 8

1 Using a sharp knife, cut the white fish fillets into serving pieces, and place them in a mixing bowl with 30ml/2 tbsp of the olive oil, the orange rind, chopped garlic, saffron threads and pastis. Turn the mixture to coat well, then cover and chill.

2 To make the rouille, first soak the breadcrumbs in a bowl of cold water, then squeeze them till they are dry. Place the breadcrumbs in a food processor or blender with the chopped garlic, roasted red pepper and tomato purée and process until it forms a smooth mixture.

3 With the food processor or blender machine running, slowly pour the olive oil through the feed tube, scraping down the sides once or twice. Set aside while you cook the fish.

4 To finish the bouillabaisse, heat the remaining 15ml/1 tbsp of olive oil in a wide flameproof casserole over a medium heat. Cook the fennel bulb and onion for about 5 minutes until the onion just softens, then add the stock.

5 Bring to the boil, add the potatoes and cook for about 5–7 minutes. Reduce the heat back to medium and begin to add the fish, starting with the thickest pieces and adding the thinner ones after 2–3 minutes. Add the prawns and continue to simmer very gently until all the fish and shellfish are fully cooked.

6 Transfer the fish, shellfish and potatoes to a heated tureen or individual soup plates. Adjust the seasoning to taste and ladle the soup over. Serve with croûtons spread with the rouille.

SPANISH SEAFOOD PAELLA

aella is probably Spain's most famous dish. This recipe creates a delicious and wholesome seafood main course dish.

INGREDIENTS
60ml/4 tbsp olive oil
225g/8oz monkfish or cod, skinned and cut into chunks
3 prepared baby squid, body cut into rings and tentacles chopped
1 red mullet, filleted, skinned and cut into chunks (optional)
1 onion, chopped
3 garlic cloves, finely chopped
1 red pepper, seeded and sliced
4 tomatoes, skinned and chopped
225g/8oz/1¼ cups arborio rice
450ml/¾ pint/1⅞ cups fish stock
150ml/¼ pint/⅔ cup white wine
75g/3oz/¾ cup frozen peas
4–5 saffron strands, steeped in 30ml/2 tbsp hot water
115g/4oz/1 cup cooked, peeled prawns
8 fresh mussels in shells, scrubbed
salt and freshly ground black pepper
15ml/1 tbsp chopped fresh parsley, to garnish
lemon wedges, to serve

SERVES 4

1 Heat 30ml/2 tbsp of the olive oil in a large frying pan and add the fish and squid to the pan. Stir-fry for 2 minutes, then transfer to a mixing bowl with all the juices and reserve till needed.

2 Heat the remaining 30ml/2 tbsp of olive oil in the frying pan and add the chopped onion, garlic and red pepper. Fry for about 6–7 minutes, stirring frequently, until the onions and peppers have softened.

3 Stir in the chopped tomatoes and fry for 2 minutes, then add the arborio rice, stirring to coat the grains with oil, and cook for 2–3 minutes. Pour on the fish stock and wine and add the peas, saffron and water. Season well and mix.

4 Gently stir in the reserved cooked fish, with all the juices, and the prawns.

5 Having made sure that the mussels are clean and free of sand by scrubbing and rinsing in several changes of water, push them into the rice. Cover and cook over a gentle heat for about 30 minutes, or until the stock has been absorbed but the mixture is still moist.

6 Remove from the heat, keep covered and leave to stand for 5 minutes. Sprinkle with parsley and serve with lemon wedges.

FRESH TUNA AND TOMATO STEW

This is a deliciously simple stew that relies on good basic ingredients. For a real Italian flavour, serve it with polenta or pasta.

INGREDIENTS
12 baby onions, peeled
900g/2lb ripe tomatoes
675g/1½lb fresh tuna
45ml/3 tbsp olive oil
2 garlic cloves, crushed
45ml/3 tbsp chopped fresh herbs
2 bay leaves
2.5ml/½ tsp caster sugar
30ml/2 tbsp sun-dried tomato purée
150ml/¼ pint/⅔ cup dry white wine
salt and freshly ground black pepper
baby courgettes and fresh herbs,
to garnish

SERVES 4

1 Leave the onions whole and cook them in a pan of boiling water for 4–5 minutes until softened. Drain.

2 Plunge the tomatoes into boiling water for 30 seconds, then refresh them in cold water. Peel away the skins and chop roughly.

3 Cut the tuna into 2.5cm/1in chunks. Heat the olive oil in a large frying or sauté pan and quickly fry the tuna until browned. Drain.

4 Add the onions, tomatoes, garlic, chopped herbs, bay leaves, sugar, sun-dried tomato purée and wine and bring the mixture to the boil, breaking up the tomatoes with a wooden spoon as it cooks.

5 Reduce the heat and simmer the stew gently for about 5 minutes. Add the cooked tuna chunks to the saucepan and cook for a further 5 minutes. Add salt and black pepper to taste, then serve the stew hot, garnished with baby courgettes and fresh herbs.

MOULES MARINIÈRE

This is the best and easiest way to serve the small tender mussels, or *bouchots*, that are farmed along much of the French coastline. Serve with plenty of crusty bread to dip in the juices.

INGREDIENTS
1.75kg/4¹/₂lb mussels
300ml/¹/₂ pint/1¹/₄ cups dry white wine
4–6 large shallots, finely chopped
bouquet garni
freshly ground black pepper

SERVES 4

1 Discard any broken mussels and those with open shells that refuse to close when tapped. Under cold running water, scrape the mussel shells with a knife to remove any barnacles and pull out the stringy "beards". Soak the mussels in several changes of cold water for at least 1 hour.

2 In a large heavy-based flameproof casserole, combine the wine, shallots, bouquet garni and plenty of black pepper. Bring to a boil over a medium-high heat and cook for 2 minutes.

3 Add the mussels and cook, tightly covered, for about 5 minutes, or until the mussels open, shaking and tossing the pan occasionally. Discard any mussels that do not open.

4 Using a slotted spoon, divide the cooked mussels among individual warmed soup plates. Tilt the casserole a little and hold it for a few seconds to allow any sand to settle to the bottom.

5 Spoon or pour the cooking liquid over the mussels, dividing it evenly, then serve at once.

MEDITERRANEAN BAKED FISH

his fish bake, *Poisson au Souquet*, is said to have originated with the fishermen on the Côte d'Azur who would cook the remains of their catch for lunch in the still-warm baker's oven.

INGREDIENTS
3 potatoes
2 onions, halved and sliced
30ml/2 tbsp olive oil, plus extra
for drizzling
2 garlic cloves, very finely chopped
675g/1¹/₂lb thick skinless fish fillets,
such as turbot or sea bass
1 bay leaf
1 thyme sprig
3 tomatoes, peeled and thinly sliced
30ml/2 tbsp orange juice
60ml/4 tbsp dry white wine
2.5ml/¹/₂ tsp saffron strands, steeped in
60ml/4 tbsp boiling water
salt and freshly ground black pepper

SERVES 4

1 Cook the potatoes in boiling salted water for 15 minutes, then drain. When the potatoes are cool enough to handle, peel off the skins and slice them thinly.

2 Meanwhile, in a heavy-based frying pan, fry the onions in the oil over a medium-low heat for about 10 minutes, stirring frequently. Add the garlic and continue cooking for a few minutes until the onions are soft and golden.

3 Preheat the oven to 190°C/375°F/Gas 5. Layer half of the cooked potato slices in a 2 litre/3¹/₃ pint/8 cup baking dish. Cover with half the onions and season well.

4 Place the fish fillets on top of the vegetables and tuck the herbs in between them. Top with the tomato slices and then the remaining onions and potatoes.

5 Pour over the orange juice, white wine and saffron liquid, season with salt and black pepper and drizzle a little extra olive oil on top. Bake the fish uncovered for about 30 minutes, until the potatoes are tender and the fish is cooked.

40

GRILLED KING PRAWNS WITH ROMESCO SAUCE

his sauce, from the Catalan region of Spain, is served with fish and seafood. Its main ingredients are pimiento, tomatoes, garlic and almonds.

INGREDIENTS
24 raw king prawns
30–45ml/2–3 tbsp olive oil
flat leaf parsley, to garnish
lemon wedges, to serve

FOR THE SAUCE
2 well-flavoured tomatoes
60ml/4 tbsp olive oil
1 onion, chopped
4 garlic cloves, chopped
1 canned pimiento, chopped
2.5ml/¹/₂ tsp dried chilli flakes or powder
75ml/5 tbsp fish stock
30ml/2 tbsp white wine
10 blanched almonds
15ml/1 tbsp red wine vinegar
salt

SERVES 4

1 To make the sauce, immerse the tomatoes in boiling water for 30 seconds, then refresh them under cold water. Peel away the skins and roughly chop the flesh.

2 Heat 30ml/2 tbsp of the oil in a pan, add the onion and 3 of the garlic cloves and cook until soft. Add the pimiento, tomatoes, chilli, fish stock and wine, then cover and simmer for 30 minutes.

3 Toast the almonds under the grill until golden. Transfer to a blender or food processor and grind coarsely. Add the remaining oil and garlic and the vinegar. Process until mixed. Add the tomato sauce and process until smooth. Season with salt.

4 Remove the heads only from the prawns and, with a sharp knife, slit each one down the back and remove the dark vein. Rinse and pat dry on kitchen paper.

5 Preheat the grill. Toss the prawns in olive oil, then spread them out in the grill pan. Grill them for about 2–3 minutes on each side, until they turn pink. Arrange them on a serving platter and garnish with parsley. Serve at once with lemon wedges and the sauce in a small bowl.

GRILLED RED MULLET WITH HERBS

I n Provence, this fish is often charcoal-grilled with herbs from the region or dried fennel sticks. You can actually use a variety of firm fish for this recipe, such as trout, as long as they are small enough to cook whole.

INGREDIENTS
olive oil, for brushing
4 red mullet (225–275g/8–10oz each),
cleaned and sliced
fresh herb sprigs, such as parsley, dill,
basil or thyme
dried fennel sticks (optional)
30–45ml/2–3 tbsp pastis

SERVES 4

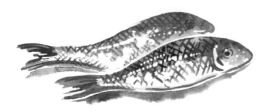

1 About 1 hour before cooking, light a charcoal fire. When ready, the coals should be grey with no flames. Generously brush a hinged grill rack with olive oil.

2 Brush each fish with a little olive oil and stuff the cavity with a few herb sprigs, breaking them to fit if necessary. Secure the fish in the grilling rack. Lay the dried fennel sticks over the coals, if using, and grill the fish for about 15–20 minutes, turning once during cooking.

3 Place the grilled mullet in a warmed flameproof serving dish. Pour the pastis into a small saucepan and heat it for about 1–2 minutes. Then tilt the saucepan and carefully ignite the liquid with a long match. Pour the pastis evenly over the fish and serve at once.

STUFFED SQUID

his Greek delicacy is best made with large squid as they are less fiddly to stuff. If you have to make do with small squid, buy about 450g/1lb.

INGREDIENTS
75ml/5 tbsp olive oil
2 large onions, finely chopped
50g/2oz/1 cup fresh breadcrumbs
2 garlic cloves, crushed
60ml/4 tbsp chopped fresh parsley
115g/4oz halloumi cheese, grated
4 squid tubes, each about 18cm/7in long
900g/2lb ripe tomatoes
5ml/1 tsp caster sugar
120ml/4fl oz/1/2 cup dry white wine
several rosemary sprigs
salt and freshly ground black pepper
toasted pine nuts and flat leaf parsley, to garnish

SERVES 4

1 To make the stuffing, heat 45ml/3 tbsp of the olive oil in a large frying pan and fry one of the onions for 3 minutes. Turn off the heat and add the breadcrumbs, garlic, parsley, cheese and seasoning. Stir well.

2 Dry the squid tubes on kitchen paper and fill with the prepared stuffing using a teaspoon. Secure the ends of the squid tubes with wooden cocktail sticks.

3 Plunge the tomatoes into boiling water for 30 seconds, then refresh in cold water. Peel away the skins and chop roughly.

4 Heat the remaining oil in a frying pan or sauté pan. Add the squid and fry on all sides, then remove them from the pan.

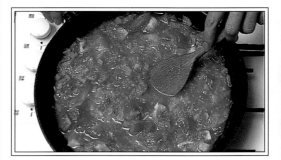

5 Add the other chopped onion to the pan and fry gently for 3 minutes. Stir in the tomatoes, sugar and wine and cook rapidly until the mixture becomes thick and pulpy.

6 Return the squid to the pan with the rosemary. Cover and cook gently for 30 minutes. Slice the squid and serve on individual plates with the sauce. Scatter over the pine nuts and garnish with parsley.

CHICKEN WITH OLIVES

F or *Poulet à la Provençale*, chicken or turkey breasts, veal or pork escalopes may be flattened for quick and even cooking. You can buy them ready-prepared in France, but they are easy to do at home as this recipe shows.

INGREDIENTS
*4 skinless boneless chicken breasts
(about 150–175g/5–6oz each)
1.5ml/¼ tsp cayenne pepper
75–105ml/5–7 tbsp extra virgin olive oil
1 garlic clove, finely chopped
16–24 black olives, stoned
6 ripe plum tomatoes, peeled and chopped
small handful fresh basil leaves
salt*

SERVES 4

1 Carefully remove the fillets (the long finger-shaped muscle on the back of each breast) and reserve for another use.

2 Place each chicken breast between two sheets of greaseproof paper or clear film. Pound with the flat side of a meat hammer or roll out with a rolling pin to flatten to about 1cm/½in in thickness. Season with salt and the cayenne pepper.

3 Heat 45–60ml/3–4 tbsp of the olive oil in a large heavy-based frying pan over a medium-high heat. Add the chicken pieces and cook for 8–10 minutes until golden brown and just cooked, turning once. Transfer the chicken to warmed serving plates and keep warm while you cook the olives and tomatoes.

4 Wipe out the frying pan and return to the heat. Add another 30–45ml/2–3 tbsp of olive oil and fry the garlic for 1 minute until golden and fragrant. Stir in the olives, cook for a further 1 minute, then stir in the tomatoes. Shred the basil leaves and stir into the olive and tomato mixture, then spoon it over the chicken and serve at once.

CHICKEN WITH LEMON AND GARLIC

E xtremely easy to cook and delicious to eat, this Spanish dish is served with fried potatoes and aïoli.

INGREDIENTS
225g/8oz skinless chicken breast fillets
30ml/2 tbsp olive oil
1 shallot, finely chopped
4 garlic cloves, finely chopped
5ml/1 tsp paprika
juice of 1 lemon
30ml/2 tbsp chopped fresh parsley
salt and freshly ground black pepper
flat leaf parsley, to garnish
lemon wedges, to serve

SERVES 4

COOK'S TIP
For a variation on this dish, try using strips of turkey breast or pork.

1 Sandwich the chicken breasts between two sheets of greaseproof paper or clear film. Pound with the flat side of a meat hammer or roll out with a rolling pin until the fillets are about 5mm/¼in thick.

2 Cut the chicken into strips about 1cm/½in wide. Heat the oil in a large frying pan. Stir-fry the chicken strips with the shallot, garlic and paprika over a high heat for about 6–8 minutes, until lightly browned and cooked through. Add the lemon juice and parsley with salt and pepper to taste. Garnish with parsley and serve hot with lemon wedges.

MOUSSAKA

ike many popular classics, a real moussaka bears little resemblance to the imitations served in Greek tourist resorts. This one is mildly spiced, moist but not dripping in grease, and encased in a golden baked crust.

INGREDIENTS
900g/2lb aubergines
120ml/4fl oz/½ cup olive oil
2 large tomatoes
2 large onions, sliced
450g/1lb minced lamb
1.5ml/¼ tsp ground cinnamon
1.5ml/¼ tsp ground allspice
30ml/2 tbsp tomato purée
45ml/3 tbsp chopped fresh parsley
120ml/4fl oz/½ cup dry white wine
salt and freshly ground black pepper

FOR THE SAUCE
50g/2oz/4 tbsp butter
50g/2oz/½ cup plain flour
600ml/1 pint/2½ cups milk
1.5ml/¼ tsp grated nutmeg
25g/1oz/⅓ cup grated Parmesan cheese
45ml/3 tbsp toasted breadcrumbs

SERVES 6

1 Cut the aubergines into 5mm/¼in thick slices. Layer them in a colander, sprinkle with plenty of salt and leave for 30 minutes.

2 Rinse the aubergine slices in several changes of cold water. Squeeze gently with your fingers to remove the excess water, then pat them dry.

3 Heat some of the oil in a large frying pan. Fry the aubergine slices in batches until golden on both sides, adding oil if needed. Leave them to drain on kitchen paper.

4 Plunge the tomatoes into boiling water for 30 seconds, then refresh in cold water. Peel away the skins and chop roughly.

5 Preheat the oven to 180°C/350°F/Gas 4. Heat 30ml/2 tbsp olive oil in a saucepan. Add the onions and minced lamb and fry gently for 5 minutes, stirring and breaking up the lamb with a wooden spoon.

6 Add the chopped tomatoes, cinnamon, allspice, tomato purée, parsley, wine and pepper and bring to the boil. Reduce the heat, cover with a lid and simmer gently for 15 minutes.

7 Arrange alternate layers of the aubergine slices and meat mixture into a shallow ovenproof dish, finishing with aubergines.

8 To make the sauce, melt the butter in a small saucepan and stir in the flour. Cook, stirring, for 1 minute. Remove from the heat and gradually blend in the milk. Return the sauce to the heat and cook, stirring, for 2 minutes or until it thickens. Add the grated nutmeg, Parmesan cheese and some salt and pepper.

9 Pour the sauce over the aubergine slices and sprinkle with the toasted breadcrumbs. Bake for 45 minutes until golden and serve hot.

CASSEROLED RABBIT WITH THYME

his is the sort of satisfying home cooking found in farmhouse kitchens and cosy neighbourhood restaurants throughout France, where rabbit is treated very much like chicken and enjoyed frequently.

INGREDIENTS

1.2kg/2½lb rabbit
40g/1½oz/¼ cup plain flour
15ml/1 tbsp butter
15ml/1 tbsp olive oil
250ml/8fl oz/1 cup red wine
350–475ml/12–16fl oz/1½–2 cups
chicken stock
15ml/1 tbsp fresh thyme leaves, or
10ml/2 tsp dried thyme
1 bay leaf
2 garlic cloves, finely chopped
10–15ml/2–3 tsp Dijon mustard
salt and freshly ground black pepper
mashed potato, to serve

SERVES 4

1 Cut the rabbit into eight serving pieces. Chop the saddle in half and separate the back legs into two pieces each, leaving the front legs whole.

2 Put the flour in a polythene bag and season it with salt and black pepper. One at a time, drop the prepared rabbit pieces into the bag and shake well to coat them with flour. Tap off any excess, then discard any remaining flour.

3 Melt the butter with the oil over a medium-high heat in a large flameproof casserole. Add the rabbit pieces and cook until they are golden, turning them so that they colour evenly.

4 Add the wine and boil for 1 minute, then add enough of the stock just to cover the meat. Add the herbs and garlic, then cover and simmer gently for 1 hour, or until the rabbit pieces are very tender and the juices run clear when the thickest part of the meat is pierced with a knife.

5 Stir in the mustard, adjust the seasoning and strain the sauce. Arrange the rabbit pieces on a warmed serving platter with some sauce and mashed potato.

SKEWERED LAMB WITH CORIANDER YOGURT

Although lamb is the most commonly used meat for Greek and Turkish kebabs, chicken, lean beef or pork work equally well. For colour, you can add alternate pieces of pepper, lemon or onions, although this is not traditional.

INGREDIENTS
900g/2lb lean boneless lamb
1 large onion, grated
3 bay leaves
5 thyme or rosemary sprigs
grated rind and juice of 1 lemon
2.5ml/½ tsp caster sugar
75ml/5 tbsp/⅓ cup olive oil
salt and freshly ground black pepper
sprigs of rosemary, to garnish
grilled lemon wedges, to serve

FOR THE CORIANDER YOGURT
150ml/¼ pint/⅔ cup thick natural yogurt
15ml/1 tbsp chopped fresh mint
15ml/1 tbsp chopped fresh coriander
10ml/2 tsp grated onion

SERVES 4

1 To make the coriander yogurt, mix together the yogurt, mint, coriander and grated onion. Transfer the mixture to a small serving dish and refrigerate.

2 To make the kebabs, cut the lamb into 3cm/1¼in chunks and place in a mixing bowl. Mix together the grated onion, fresh herbs, lemon rind and juice, sugar and olive oil, then add salt and black pepper and pour over the lamb.

3 Mix the meat and its marinade together and leave to marinate in the fridge for several hours or overnight.

4 Preheat the grill. Drain the meat and thread it on to skewers. Arrange the kebabs on a grill rack and cook for about 10 minutes until browned, turning occasionally. Transfer to a plate and garnish with rosemary. Serve with the grilled lemon wedges and coriander yogurt.

BOLOGNESE MEAT SAUCE

his great meat sauce is a speciality of Bologna, Italy. It is delicious with tagliatelle or short pastas, such as penne or pasta shells, as well as spaghetti, and is indispensable in baked lasagne. It keeps well in the fridge for several days and can also be frozen. Sprinkle some Parmesan cheese over the top when serving, if liked, for extra flavour.

INGREDIENTS
25g/1oz/2 tbsp butter
60ml/4 tbsp olive oil
1 onion, finely chopped
25g/1oz/2 tbsp pancetta or unsmoked
bacon, finely chopped
1 carrot, finely sliced
1 celery stick, finely sliced
1 clove garlic, finely chopped
350g/12oz lean minced beef
150ml/¼ pint/⅔ cup red wine
120ml/4fl oz/½ cup milk
400g/14oz can plum tomatoes,
chopped, with their juice
1 bay leaf
2.5ml/½ tsp fresh thyme leaves
salt and freshly ground black pepper
cooked spaghetti, to serve

FOR 6 SERVINGS OF PASTA

1 Heat the butter and oil in a heavy pan or earthenware pot. Add the onion and cook over a moderate heat for 3–4 minutes. Add the pancetta and cook until the onion is translucent. Stir in the carrot, celery and garlic. Cook for 3–4 minutes more.

2 Add the minced beef, and crumble it into the vegetables with a fork. Stir it until the meat loses its red colour. Season with salt and pepper.

3 Pour in the wine, raise the heat slightly, and cook until the liquid evaporates, for about 3–4 minutes. Add the milk and cook until it evaporates.

4 Stir in the tomatoes with their juice and the herbs. Bring the sauce to the boil. Reduce the heat to low and simmer, uncovered, for 1½–2 hours, stirring occasionally. Correct the seasoning before serving with spaghetti, or other pasta.

ROAST LOIN OF PORK STUFFED WITH FIGS, OLIVES AND ALMONDS

Pork is a popular meat in Spain and this recipe, using fruit and nuts in the stuffing, is of Catalan influence, where the combination of meat and fruit is quite common.

INGREDIENTS
60ml/4 tbsp olive oil
1 onion, finely chopped
2 cloves garlic, chopped
75g/3oz/1¹/₂ cups fresh breadcrumbs
4 ready-to-eat dried figs, chopped
8 green olives, stoned and chopped
25g/1oz/¹/₄ cup flaked almonds
15ml/1 tbsp lemon juice
15ml/1 tbsp chopped fresh parsley
1 egg yolk
900g/2lb boned loin of pork
salt and freshly ground black pepper

SERVES 4

COOK'S TIP
Keep a tub of breadcrumbs in the freezer. They can be used frozen.

1 Preheat the oven to 200°C/400°F/Gas 6. Heat 45ml/3 tbsp of the oil in a pan, add the onion and garlic and cook gently until softened. Remove the pan from the heat and stir in the breadcrumbs, figs, chopped olives, flaked almonds, lemon juice, parsley and egg yolk. Season to taste.

2 Remove any string from the pork and unroll the belly flap, cutting away any excess fat or meat to enable you to do so. Spread half the stuffing over the flat piece and roll it up, starting from the thick side. Tie it at intervals with string.

3 Pour the remaining oil into a small roasting tin and place the pork in it. Roast the pork in the preheated oven for 1 hour 15–45 minutes, until cooked through. Shape the remaining stuffing mixture into even-size balls and add them to the roasting tin around the meat, 15–20 minutes before the end of the cooking time.

4 Remove the pork from the oven and let it rest for 10 minutes. Carve it into thick slices and serve with the stuffing balls and any juices from the tin. This dish is also good served cold.

BAKED LASAGNE WITH MEAT SAUCE

his lasagne, made from fresh pasta with home-made meat and béchamel sauces, is a classic dish.

INGREDIENTS
1 recipe Bolognese Meat Sauce
400g/14oz fresh lasagne
115g/4oz/1 cup grated Parmesan cheese
40g/1½oz/3 tbsp butter

FOR THE BÉCHAMEL SAUCE
750ml/1¼ pints/3 cups milk
1 bay leaf
3 blades mace
115g/4oz/½ cup butter
75g/3oz/¼ cup flour
salt and freshly ground black pepper

SERVES 8–10

1 Prepare the meat sauce and set it aside. Butter a large shallow baking dish, preferably rectangular or square.

2 Make the béchamel sauce by gently heating the milk with the bay leaf and mace in a small saucepan. Melt the butter in a heavy-based saucepan. Add the flour, and mix it in well with a wire whisk. Cook for 2–3 minutes.

3 Strain the hot milk into the flour and butter, and mix smoothly with a whisk. Bring the sauce to the boil, stirring constantly, and cook for 4–5 minutes more. Season with salt and pepper, and set aside.

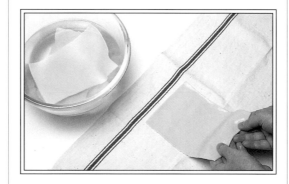

4 Preheat the oven to 200°C/400°F/Gas 6. Bring a large pan of water to the boil and add salt. Drop in 3–4 pasta rectangles and cook them for about 30 seconds. Remove with a slotted spoon, and drop them into a bowl of cold water. Take them out, shaking off the excess water, and lay them out flat, without overlapping, on a teacloth. Repeat for the remaining pasta.

5 To assemble the lasagne, have the baking dish, béchamel and meat sauces, pasta strips, grated Parmesan and butter at hand. Spread a large spoonful of the meat sauce over the bottom of the dish. Arrange a layer of pasta on top, cutting it so that it fits well inside the dish.

6 Cover with a thin layer of meat sauce, then one of béchamel. Sprinkle with a little cheese. Repeat, making up to six pasta layers, ending with a layer of pasta coated with béchamel. Sprinkle with Parmesan and dot with butter.

7 Bake the lasagne in the preheated oven for 20 minutes or until it is brown on top. Remove and allow to stand for about 5 minutes before serving. Serve from the baking dish, cutting out rectangular or square sections for each helping. Lasagne is also delicious served cold.

TIRAMISÙ

Tiramisù means "pick me up", and this rich egg and coffee dessert is guaranteed to do just that!

INGREDIENTS
500g/1¼lb mascarpone cheese
5 eggs, separated, at room temperature
90g/3½oz/scant ½ cup caster sugar
pinch of salt
sponge fingers or slices of sponge cake, to line dish(es)
120ml/4fl oz/½ cup strong Italian espresso coffee
60ml/4 tbsp brandy or rum (optional)
cocoa powder, to sprinkle

SERVES 6–8

COOK'S TIP
Mascarpone cheese has a delicate flavour and is ideal for desserts. It can be found in most large supermarkets and Italian delicatessens.

---

1 Beat the mascarpone cheese in a small bowl until soft. In a separate bowl, beat the egg yolks with the sugar (reserving 15ml/1 tbsp) until the mixture is pale yellow and fluffy. Gradually beat in the cheese.

2 Using an electric beater or wire whisk, beat the egg whites with the salt until they form stiff peaks. Fold the egg whites into the mascarpone mixture.

3 Line one large or several individual serving dishes with the sponge fingers or slices. Add the reserved sugar to the coffee and stir in the alcohol, if using.

4 Sprinkle the espresso coffee over the sponge slices in the dish(es) so that they become moist, but not saturated. Cover them with half of the egg mixture. Make another layer of sponge slices moistened with espresso and cover with the remaining egg mixture. Sprinkle with cocoa powder. Leave in the fridge for at least 1 hour, preferably more, before serving.

ORANGE RICE PUDDING

In Spain, Greece, Italy and Morocco rice puddings are a favourite dish, especially when sweetened with honey and flavoured with orange.

INGREDIENTS
50g/2oz/¼ cup short-grain pudding rice
600ml/1 pint/2½ cups milk
30–45ml/2–3 tbsp clear honey,
according to taste
finely grated rind of ½ small orange
150ml/¼ pint/⅔ cup double cream
15ml/1 tbsp chopped pistachio
nuts, toasted, to decorate

SERVES 4

1 Mix the rice with the milk, honey and orange rind in a saucepan and bring to the boil, then reduce the heat, cover and simmer very gently for about 1¼ hours, stirring regularly.

2 Remove the lid from the saucepan and continue cooking and stirring the mixture for about 15–20 minutes, or until the rice is creamy.

3 Pour in the double cream and simmer for 5–8 minutes longer. Serve the rice sprinkled with the pistachio nuts in individual warmed bowls, or serve chilled.

BAKLAVA

This sweet and spicy pie from Greece and Turkey is made with layers of buttered filo pastry, packed with nuts and sweetened with a honey and lemon syrup.

INGREDIENTS
75g/3oz/6 tbsp butter, melted
6 large sheets of filo pastry
225g/8oz/2 cups chopped mixed nuts,
such as almonds, pistachios, hazelnuts
and walnuts
50g/2oz/1 cup fresh breadcrumbs
5ml/1 tsp ground cinnamon
5ml/1 tsp mixed spice
2.5ml/½ tsp grated nutmeg
250ml/8fl oz/1 cup clear honey
60ml/4 tbsp lemon juice

MAKES 10 PIECES

1 Preheat the oven to 180°C/350°F/Gas 4. Butter a 18 x 28cm/7 x 11in tin. Unroll the pastry, brush one sheet with melted butter (keep the remainder covered with a dish towel while you work) and use it to line the tin, easing it carefully up the sides.

2 Brush two more sheets of pastry with butter and lay them on top of the base sheet, easing the pastry into the corners and letting the edges overhang.

3 Mix together the nuts, breadcrumbs and spices in a bowl and spoon this mixture into the lined tin.

4 Cut the remaining three sheets of filo pastry in half widthways and brush each one with a little of the butter. Layer the sheets on top of the filling and fold in any overhanging edges.

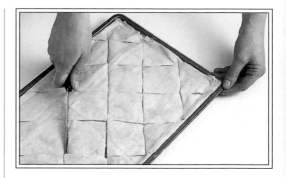

5 Top with the remaining buttered sheets of pastry. Cut the baklava diagonally into diamonds. Bake in the preheated oven for about 30 minutes, until golden.

6 Meanwhile, heat the honey and lemon juice together in a pan. When the baklava is cooked, remove it from the oven and pour the syrup over while still warm. Leave to cool completely, re-cut into diamonds and serve.

CHOCOLATE ICE CREAM

se good-quality plain or cooking chocolate for the best flavour in this classic *gelato* recipe.

INGREDIENTS
900ml/1¹/₂ pints/scant 3³/₄ cups milk
10cm/4in piece of vanilla pod
4 egg yolks
90g/3¹/₂oz/¹/₂ cup sugar
225g/8oz cooking chocolate, melted

MAKES ABOUT 3³/₄ CUPS

VARIATION
To make Custard Ice Cream, replace the vanilla pod with 2.5 ml/½ tsp grated lemon zest, and use 6 egg yolks. Leave out the chocolate.

1 Make a custard by heating the milk with the vanilla pod in a small saucepan. Do not let the milk boil.

2 Beat the egg yolks with a wire whisk or electric beater. Gradually incorporate the sugar, and continue beating for 5 minutes, or until the mixture turns pale yellow. Strain the milk and slowly add it to the egg mixture gradually.

3 Pour the mixture and the chocolate into a bowl placed over a pan of simmering water. Stir over a moderate heat until the water in the pan is boiling, and the custard thickens to lightly coat the back of a spoon. Remove from the heat and allow to cool.

4 Freeze the chocolate ice cream in an ice cream maker, or place it in a freezer container. Freeze for 3 hours, chop and process, then return to the freezer. Repeat this process 2–3 times until a smooth consistency has been reached.

HALVA

 he Greeks love home-made halva which they cook in a saucepan with semolina, olive oil, sugar, honey and almonds. You can either eat it warm, or allow it to set and then cut it into slices or squares.

INGREDIENTS
400g/14oz/2 cups sugar
1 litre/1³/4 pints/4 cups water
2 cinnamon sticks
250ml/8fl oz/1 cup olive oil
350g/12oz/3 cups semolina
75g/3oz/³/4 cup blanched almonds,
6–8 halved, the rest chopped
120ml/4fl oz/¹/2 cup clear honey
ground cinnamon, to serve

MAKES 12–16 PIECES

1 Reserve 2oz/¼ cup of the sugar and dissolve the rest in the water over a gentle heat, stirring from time to time.

2 Add the cinnamon sticks, bring to the boil, then simmer for 5 minutes. Cool and remove the cinnamon sticks.

3 Heat the olive oil in a heavy-based saucepan and, when it is quite hot, stir in the semolina. Cook, stirring occasionally, until it turns golden brown, then add the chopped almonds and cook for a further minute or so.

4 Keep the heat low and stir in the prepared sugar syrup, taking care as the semolina may spit. Bring the mixture to the boil, stirring it constantly. When it is just smooth, remove the pan from the heat and stir in the honey.

5 Allow to cool slightly, then mix in the reserved sugar. Pour the halva into a greased and lined shallow pan, pat it down and mark into 12–16 squares.

6 Sprinkle the halva lightly with ground cinnamon and fix one almond half on each square. When set, cut up and serve.

HONEY AND PINE NUT TART

onderful tarts of all descriptions are to be found throughout France, and this recipe recalls the flavours of the south.

INGREDIENTS
FOR THE PASTRY
225g/8oz/2 cups plain flour
115g/4oz/¹/₂ cup butter
30ml/2 tbsp icing sugar
1 egg
icing sugar, for dusting
vanilla ice cream, to serve (optional)

FOR THE FILLING
115g/4oz/¹/₂ cup unsalted butter, diced
115g/4oz/¹/₂ cup caster sugar
3 eggs, beaten
*175g/6oz/²/₃ cup sunflower or
other flower honey*
grated rind and juice of 1 lemon
225g/8oz/2²/₃ cups pine nuts
pinch of salt

SERVES 6

1 Preheat the oven to 180°C/350°F/Gas 4. Sift the flour into a bowl, add the butter and work with your fingertips until the mixture resembles fine breadcrumbs. Stir in the icing sugar. Add the egg and 15ml/1 tbsp of water and work to a firm dough that leaves the bowl clean.

2 Roll out the pastry on a floured surface and use it to line a 23cm/9in tart tin. Prick the base all over with a fork, and chill for 10 minutes. Line with foil or greaseproof paper and fill with dried beans or rice, or baking beans if you have them. Bake the tart case for 10 minutes.

3 Cream together the butter and caster sugar until light. Beat in the eggs little by little. Gently heat the honey in a small saucepan until runny, then add to the butter mixture with the lemon rind and juice. Stir in the pine nuts and salt, then pour the filling into the pastry case.

4 Bake the tart in the preheated oven for about 45 minutes, or until the filling is lightly browned and set. Leave it to cool slightly in the tin, before dusting it quite generously with icing sugar. Serve the tart warm, or at room temperature, with vanilla ice cream, if liked.

INDEX